DONALD TRUMP

Servant of Jesus Christ or of satan?

Have we been deceived? Judge for yourself!

Dr. Robbi Warren

Donald Trump: Servant of Jesus Christ, or of satan?

Unless otherwise noted, all Scripture quotations are taken from the King James Version of the The Holy Bible.

Scripture quotations marked (AMP) are taken from the Holy Bible, Amplified. Old Testament Copyright © 1965, 1987 by The Zondervan Corporation, Grand Rapids, Michigan. The Amplified New Testament Copyright © 1954, 1958, 1987 by The Lockman Foundation. Used by permission.

Scripture quotations marked (NIV) are taken from the Holy Bible, New International Version. NIV Copyright © 1973, 1978, 1984 by International Bible Society. Used by permission by Zondervan. All rights reserved.

Sources include Wikipedia, Britannica, the Library of Congress and limited assistance from A.I. / ChatGPT.

 For more information, write: Robbi Warren International Ministries, PO Box 724, Upper Marlboro MD 20773. (800) 478-4225.
rwministry@netscape.net

ISBN 979-8-218-96670-6 (paperback)
ISBN 979-0-9708982-8-9 (hardcover)

Printed in the United States of America

Dedication

This book is dedicated to the memory of my paternal grandparents, Lawrence and Dorothy Warren, who raised me from the age of five months old, and adopted me when I was around 11 or 12, and raised me in the fear of the Lord.

Also to my biological Mother and Father who brought me into this world; William, Sr. and Mary Francis Warren.

And to my great-grandparents Frank and Mamie McClain. Thanks for investing so much in my life as a kid.

I also want to dedicate this book to those who have blessed me spiritually and naturally on this Journey: my Pastors, Spiritual Mothers and Fathers. Pastor Earl Jackson, Sr.; Pastor Willie and Dorothy Perkins; Pastor James Kilgore; Mother Narvie Green; Bishop Willie Smith; Pastor Winnie Gilliam; Bishop James Nelson, Sr.; Bishop James Tyson; Bishop Chandler D. Owens; Bishop George McKinney; my sister T Carter; my brother Jack; and to all the Pastors who have opened their church doors for me to flow in the Holy Spirit. My music producers Jonathan Dubose, Jr., and my mentor, Pastor Andraé Crouch; Terry, Greg and my WATC fam; Kevin and my fam; The Word Network and my television production guy, Fred Windham R.I.P.

And to my Lord and Savior, Jesus Christ. To God be the Glory.

Disclaimer

Before, or after, reading this book, I pray that the message does not get lost in the climate of politics. Nor the bias of one side against the other. As a born-again believer, I'm looking at things from a biblical and spiritual perspective, not a biased one.

It's clear to some that former President Donald J. Trump doesn't like to lose. It's obvious to others that he craves more power. These are among the characteristics of lucifer and will be the manifestation of the diabolical *anti*christ spirit. I'm not saying that Donald Trump *is* the antichrist. But, some of the things that he has said and done – and continues to say and do – reflect that spirit. And it's not just him, but others who seem to be under the influence of that spirit. This includes some church leaders as well as secular leaders and people in general. Keep in mind: satan and his demons know this. Therefore, they also know that their time – as well as mankind's – is short.

And in these last days, their main assignment is to deceive the whole world. The great deceiver (satan) is always looking for people he can use as a tool to carry out his deceptive plans. Always remember, it's appointed unto man once to die, but after death comes the Judgment. That means, ending up in heaven or hell (lake of fire), as we as believers believe, no matter what our political affiliation or the color of our skin. We got a date with judgment.

Let me say this again: any of us can become a tool of satan. The devil and his demons are looking for a physical body in order to carry out their plan. Don't let it be you!

Now you know! That's what the intention of this book is all about. Judge for yourself!

Table of Contents

About the Author

Dr. Robbi Warren (Robbi Warren) was raised by his grandparents since he was a baby. They eventually became his legal parents by way of adoption. They taught him – and showed him, by example – what it meant to be compassionate, concerned and considerate of others. They also taught him how to be observant and to be a critical thinker.

Young Robbi watched his parents work hard, building a beauty salon from the ground up in their small, multi-cultural community. His mother, being a beautician, was also an accomplished pianist who taught piano lessons. His father was a hard-working truck driver and his great-grandfather owned his own trucking company. He watched his family buy rental property in the late 60s so that others would have a decent place to live. And when renters often couldn't pay, his parents refused to evict them. His parents also bought a van and a station wagon so that kids in town would have transportation to school while their parents worked. All of this made a lasting impact on him, molding his life to be selfless and sensitive to all races, rather than being selfish and self-centered.

In his school years, he was an athlete who also held several jobs. He worked in retail (both clothing and shoe stores), as well as in a pharmacy. He learned that it takes hard work to be productive in life. He also realized how precious life could be. When during his freshman year of high school, one of his dear friends, who was a star athlete, died in a horrific car accident with his niece. They both were thrown through the windshield of the car in which they were riding in. At their funeral, he realized, at a very young age, how fragile life could be. He also realized his need for a real relationship with Jesus Christ and soon after became a born-again believer. He had always been a churchgoer because of his mom being the Minister of Music at various churches and his dad being one of the deacons.

After graduation, he started working in the construction business with his biological father, who was a foreman at a construction company. Still in his teens, he was determined to work as hard, if not harder, then the grown men who were much older than him.

One day, he heard the Holy Ghost tell him to go visit his biological mom, who he hadn't seen in years. He prayed to God for confirmation, asking that if this is what God wanted him to do, to let his father lay him off the construction job. And when that happened, he immediately bought a one-way bus ticket to Florida. Keep in mind, he was still just a teenager, fresh out of high school, and had never been away from his adoptive parents. They were extremely upset and not in favor of him leaving.

But he obeyed Jesus Christ over his parents. Riding the bus by himself, from the small town of Lockhart, Texas to another small town in Crestview, Florida, where he didn't know anyone but his biological mother, was a very uncomfortable experience. But he had heard from Jesus Christ and that's where the manifestation of ministry came to light. After meeting a pastor and his wife at a church that he visited for the first time, the pastor's wife of the First Church of God in Christ asked him to speak to the young people. Even though he had not acknowledged any call to preach, and was only 18 years old, he accepted the invitation. The first time he spoke, it was a disaster. And he vowed to never speak again. He had tried to do what he had seen others do, instead of what Jesus Christ wanted him to speak. The second time he was asked to speak, he realized that there was something special about his ability to communicate with others, especially young people, through delivering the Word.

The rest is history. For 40+ years, Robbi has become a voice in both the Christian and secular communities. He received a Doctor of Divinity from Eastern Bible Institute, a Bachelor from Cornerstone University and many other awards and accolades. He has established several radio and television programs around the world: WYCB, WCVG, KYOK, Love 860 and many more. Television telecasts such as BET, The WORD Network, WATC Atlanta, Far East Television and many others. He has written two books, Bit, But Not Poisoned (One and Two); recorded five music CDs, one featuring gospel legend Andraé Crouch; five motivational / transformational CDs; and thousands of cassettes, VHS, DVDs, etc.

Preface

Before making any assumptions about this book, or about me, I hope and pray you hear my heart and hear the voice of our Lord and Savior Jesus Christ.

This book is not about bashing the former President of the United States of America, Donald Trump. But it's meant to enlighten those of you who don't want to see or hear (or maybe are just willing to ignore) the spirit of deception that's going on. Even if you're not a born-again believer, deception is still real.

For instance, Donald Trump has allegedly always manifested an obsession for money and power. Yet, with all the money he claims to have – and brags constantly about how rich he is – why isn't he paying his own legal bills? That's what I want people to question, and not simply accept his deceit and deception.

With that being said, I know some are too emotionally attached (or maybe even brainwashed) to hear and see the obvious. But this book is about *you*. You spend your hard-earned money for "the Donald," while his money sits in the bank collecting interest. Why is he using a bail bonds company instead of his own money? He's selling mugs, t-shirts and other products, making millions!

Is that godly? I'm a born-again believer, too, by the way. And I *do* hear from Jesus Christ. But something is wrong with this picture.

Power, money and authority; apparently, he can't get enough. Donald Trump really needs Jesus Christ in his life. I think some will understand what I'm saying.

Where is Paula White or some of the other celebrity preachers? What kind of spiritual counsel was Donald Trump getting? My heart goes out to him. Someone should have had enough power for his deliverance.

We can't keep blaming the LGBTQ+ agenda, or the abortionists, for the decay of America and the world. Because God gave all mankind the power to *choose*. God never made anyone serve him. Think about it. Noah preached the consequences of sin for 120 years. Even in the story of Sodom and Gomorrah, folks made their own choices. The Scriptures say, "Whosoever will, let him come to Jesus Christ."

I believe that Donald Trump is using manipulative techniques directed toward the Christian community for them to believe that he is their answer (messiah).

Now you know why I wrote this book. Judge for yourself! Donald Trump, Servant of Jesus Christ, or of satan?

Introduction

Well, since I've introduced myself, let me introduce the book and the purpose of this book that's titled <u>Donald Trump, Servant of Jesus Christ, or of satan? Judge for yourself!</u>

Throughout this book, you will see some of the history of Donald Trump and his upbringing, his faith, etc. You will also read some of the history of America which has produced men like Donald Trump and myself. Keep in mind that America is only 247 years old. That means that when Donald Trump was born, America was only 170 years old. Robbi, being much younger, has researched the history of America. For some, it has been a country of dreams. But for others, it has been a country of nightmares. Laws had to be passed for people of color just to receive food, housing and better jobs. This was only about sixty or seventy years ago! And in some parts of the country, it still exists today.

The Civil Rights Act of 1964 – signed into law on July the 2nd of that year – outlawed segregation in businesses such as theaters, restaurants and hotels. It banned discriminatory practices in employment and ended segregation in public places such as swimming pools, libraries, and public schools.

Prior to that, on May 17, 1954, U.S. Supreme Court Justice Earl Warren delivered the unanimous ruling in the landmark civil rights case *Brown v. Board of Education of Topeka, Kansas*. In this milestone decision, the Supreme Court ruled that separating children in public schools on the basis of race was unconstitutional. It signaled the end of legalized racial segregation in the schools of the United States, overruling the "separate but equal" principle set forth in the 1896 *Plessy v. Ferguson* case.

Donald Trump, like many other Caucasians, grew up in this era whereby they felt that America belonged to them – the Caucasian race – and that others should serve them. They felt they were doing others a favor by letting them even be here in America. And that they could go back to Africa or wherever else they came from. Forgetting – intentionally or not – that their forefathers, too, had once come from another country.

Many still have that same superiority complex today. They believe people of color are inferior to them. This is a major problem even among some fellow Christians today. I think it's very important to consider these things as we move forward in this book.

CHAPTER ONE

The Man and His Influencers / Mentors

When people think of Donald Trump, most think of him as a man who has made an impact on the United States and the world because of his financial accomplishments. But, when you think about it, many of us don't really know him.

How did he become known as a multi-billionaire? Is it based on verifiable financial records or simply what he says?

Who were his parents? His mother and father? What about his siblings?

Not much apparently is said about Donald's mother. But we do know certain things about his father. Fred Trump, a savvy businessman in the New York area was an iconic figure, known as both a developer and a real estate mogul. Though his beginning seems to be questionable, he established himself financially by owning several apartment complexes in the New York City area.

As Fred Trump became a financial giant, he passed his genius and inheritance to his children. Donald apparently became his go-to. Later on, certain family members complained and filed a lawsuit against him concerning the family business (Mary Trump and Fred Trump III). Seeing how Donald was toward his family says a lot.

If you take the time, you will find certain articles out there that will shed light on this man. And give insight as to how he has become who he is. As well as the environment that possibly molded, or drove, him into this iconic and toxic figure (People magazine and other media).

Now, have I ever met him? No, but the Scriptures tell us, you'll know a tree by its fruit.

In Donald's early days, Fred Trump took his family to the Marble Collegiate Church in New York, which was under the pastorship of Dr. Norman Vincent Peale. Dr. Peale was a popular television and radio personality. His teaching transcended the traditional Christian life into a more New Age perspective. One of his doctrinal beliefs, according to writings, was that you must believe in yourself just as much as you believe in God.

He wrote the best-selling book, The Power of Positive Thinking, which embraced humanism and psychology as a means to get what you desire in life. Even employing some tactics of mind control, etc. This type of concept and theory was viewed by many as heresy especially if it excluded the life of Jesus Christ. And many leaders allegedly described Dr. Peale himself as a heretic. Because of his newfound beliefs.

I can picture little Donald sitting there hearing and being told, "you can be and have whatever you think or believe. You are a god. Continue to believe in yourself and you can accomplish anything. Defeat and failure are not options."

SUMMARY

As you read more about Fred Trump and Dr. Peale, in multiple media sources, you can see that they had an impact and influence on Donald Trump's life. Fred Trump mentored him in business. Dr. Peale apparently mentored his thinking with his teaching on The Power of Positive Thinking. I encourage my readers to do your own research as I did mine Judge for yourself!

CHAPTER TWO

Businessman or Con Man?

How did Donald J. Trump allegedly become a multi-billionaire?

It has been reported by many articles and sources that Donald – after working for his father and learning from him how to make money – not only inherited millions from the estate of his late father, but allegedly was able to gain part of other family member's inheritance, according to his niece Mary Trump, who sued him. Even those who worked for him oftentimes complained that they didn't get paid. What about all the bankruptcies, the business failures, the falsifications of documents, the list goes on and on?

Many have embraced his deceitful rhetoric. They either don't know it's deceitful, or they *choose* not to know. They apparently don't have a problem with anything "the Donald" says or does.

I'm doing my due diligence. Starting with defining: *What is a lie?* How does one know when a lie is being spoken or told?

Very simple for those who are objective. But those who are obsessed with the Donald will allegedly believe whatever he says. And being the showman that he is, he will intentionally feed those individuals lies and deception. The key word is *intentional*, when it comes to giving misinformation.

Always remember, there's an *art* to lying. Or being deceitful.

When Donald says things that are totally untrue, intentionally to appeal to his unwavering base, that is a clear sign of lying, deceit and deception. Always fact check what he and others are saying.

Donald Trump is also a master manipulator. Allegedly.

Do you know how liars operate?

My quest is not to attack anyone, but to expose the difference between a lie and the truth. Do you even consider when he speaks, whether he's telling the truth, or lying? Ask yourself, "Is what he's saying truth, or another lie?" Fact check. Fact check. Fact check.

If I say I'm working for *Christianity* and for your *Christian values*, how do you know for certain that I am actually doing what I'm saying? And not lying and simply baiting you to support my hidden agenda?

This man has a hidden agenda. That's what many are ignoring. It seems to be all about money and power. Those of you who claim to be of the Christian faith and lovers of Jesus Christ, are you still buying into what he's saying? How many more lies does a person have to tell?

By the way, what are Donald Trump's Christian values? Or, is it about his own agenda? Let's be honest with ourselves as human beings. Always look at the character of a man or a woman.

What about his college days at prestigious Wharton Business School? Someone allegedly stated that he paid other students to do his schoolwork for him. Is everyone lying on the Donald?

I understand the Christian religion very well. But I also know how easy it is for con men and women to lie and mislead gullible and vulnerable people to believe their lies. Our country – and the world – is in serious trouble because of this factor.

Your Bible told you it would be this way, the closer we get to the end. That people would rather believe a lie instead of the truth.

SUMMARY

Now we all know that Donald is a businessman, because some of us have seen his hotels, golf courses, former football team, his television show, "The Apprentice," and the selling of his products. But con man? Well, with all the public information concerning his business dealings that caused countless lawsuits over the years – some have been settled out of court, but where there's smoke, there's fire – it is quite clear that his business dealings have been questionable. And he has admitted to using loopholes in our laws here in America when it comes to taxes and bankruptcies. Which shows patterns and intent. Judge for yourself!

CHAPTER THREE

What Role Did Faith Play In His Life?

It's been well documented that Donald Trump's father, Fred Trump – who was a businessman, builder, real estate developer, etc. – was allegedly a member of Marble Collegiate Church under the pastorship of Dr. Norman Vincent Peale. Dr. Peale was an iconic orator and communicator of one believing in one's self.

As we again explore the teaching of Dr. Norman Vincent Peale; his brilliant way of thinking and his thought-provoking lectures, we can look deeper into the making of Donald Trump and his mindset. Now, some may ask, *why are you revisiting <u>this</u>?* Just follow me and you will see.

One of Dr. Peale's passionate beliefs was that by believing in ourselves as much as we believe in God, we become little gods. Remember he wrote the book, <u>The Power of Positive Thinking</u>.

With that being said, Fred Trump exposed his family to this teaching when they were young. Now you can see the blueprint of the two major influential individuals in Donald Trump's life: his father when it came to making money, and the guru concerning the power of positive thinking.

Well, you may say, "What's wrong with making money, or thinking positive in life?" That's a great question. But remember, the *love* of money is the root of all evil.

There is a powerful spirit, I believe, behind Donald Trump. Mankind is made up of body, soul and spirit. A triune being. And the enemy is looking for people who have opened themselves up, spiritually, so that he can use them as a tool to spread deception.

There's a difference in the natural body and the spiritual body. Oftentimes we are impressed more with the natural man (flesh) instead of the spiritual aspect of man. This is where deception takes place.

What really controls the natural man is the spirit that's influencing the natural man or woman (antichrist). Donald Trump's father took the family to the Marble Church. The pastor of the church was Dr. Norman Vincent Peale. As I explore again the onset of what took place in Donald Trump's early life, it's interesting to see how he was molded to think and to be who he is today. Can't you see that?

It seems we often overlook a person's beginning and how they were raised. Is Donald Trump, the natural man, different than the spirit behind the man? Ask yourself this question: *How is a man able to influence millions with his nonsensical behavior?*

Stay tuned in the furtherment of this chapter and I will explain.

Remember I told you how when Donald Trump was a kid his father Fred Trump took him to church along with the other family members? The teaching of Norman Vincent Peale apparently was life-changing for young Donald.

The teaching of the power of positive thinking can be divisive. Because some people will go to the extreme and not deal with reality. Think about that for one second and you will see what I am saying.

It could be good, but it can also become evil. Godly balance is very important.

Because the teaching of Dr. Peale primarily has to do with your *thoughts*, which can be evil and wicked. Your belief in yourself goes beyond just your belief in God. In other words, you can become your own personal creator.

We've already discussed Donald Trump, the man. Now, let's look at what *spirit* could be influencing him.

Once again, never underestimate the power of satan and the spirits that are under his authority that can partner with the spirit of an individual who is not fully surrendered to Jesus Christ. It is quite obvious to some of us that Donald Trump has a spirit in him that is not of God.

He has displayed such a disdain for democracy, the Constitution and fellow human beings who don't believe like him. Some people have stated emphatically that America was founded on biblical Christian principles. But what are those Christian principles and values? What are Donald Trump's Christian principles, if he has any?

I often say that America is a Christian country, but is it a godly country?

Which is a big difference.

Christianity has to do with those who followed Jesus Christ. Not necessarily applying godly principles to their lives. Anyone can become a Christian in name, in spite of their ungodly ways and willful sinning.

The term *Christianity* was written about those who followed Jesus Christ at Antioch. Today, many who claim to be of the Christian religion have not been taught nor discipled. Therefore, some have become very ungodly. They lack love and concern for one another.

Now, I may be faced with tremendous backlash because I'm willing to address the elephant in the room. For those of you who don't like truth, my advice is to stop reading what is being written.

Because, as you will see, the Bible references the deceit, hypocrisy, and the spirit of deception that is running rampant.

Some may ask, *"What do you mean?"*

I'm glad you asked. Even though the Bible speaks about slavery, it doesn't mean that Jesus Christ was okay with people who had slaves.

The Bible is full of historical customs, traditions and events. Some have even made doctrines out of these events. Which were never meant to be a universal prerequisite in order to be hateful and angry toward anyone. Nor to dictate, control, or even mistreat others who don't believe like them.

Biblical history not only gives us the essence of God, but it also gives us the history of mankind which shows their evil ways and deeds. And it shows us the judgment of God that will take place upon the world, and mankind, concerning their choices and the consequences of their rebellion toward Jesus Christ and sinful decisions.

SUMMARY

Understanding Faith can be very complex because words have various meanings. What do people really believe in? This book is written to convey information, not convince anyone of anything. Even the various sources I use and give credit to. Now I *do* believe that Donald Trump has some exposure to the Christian faith. But I doubt he's a devout believer. Just like many others. The Bible says, you'll know a tree by its fruits, implying you will know a person by the fruits of the Spirit. There you have it. Judge for yourself!

CHAPTER FOUR

The Spirit of Racism and Donald Trump

Now many that don't look like me will totally disagree that racism still exists. Some believe that America belongs to one nationality or one race of people (Caucasians).

It's important to have a clear understanding of slavery, racism and the racist mindset that some have toward those who don't look like them. And how Donald Trump is feeding into this mindset.

Make America Great Again? Some will say, he's really saying, *Make America white Again.* Listen closely to his speeches.

Now, when we look at when America was first established, did any of those who brought slaves over to this new founded land, bring them here to be *over* any of them? Many of our ancestors were slaves and those who brought them over became slave masters and brought the spirit of racism with them.

It seems that the teaching of Critical Race Theory is being banned, but the teaching of those who had slaves is still accepted as "Great Americans who contributed to the building of America" even though slaves had a lot to do with the building of America, too.

Now even though this is true, there's another side to the establishment of America. It has to do with the mistreatment of slaves and segregation.

Donald Trump knows this. And allegedly he's using this as a tool to continue to divide America.

No, this is not playing the race card. But this is a part of our history and there are those who don't want to hear it.

Bottom line: they (Caucasians) didn't bring slaves to America to be over them, but to serve them. And many allegedly look to Donald Trump to bring back white dominance and authority.

What does this mean?

White Nationalists, KKK and other groups honestly believe that America belongs to the white race. This is a fact. Donald Trump has played on this obvious division.

He has showed this by his disdain for President Barack Obama and his birth certificate. Saying he wasn't born in America and his birth certificate was fake. When it was proven that former President Obama was born in Hawaii, did Donald Trump ever apologize for his outlandish statement?

This is not just about politics. It's deeper than that. It's about what nationality will be in control. This is not a conspiracy theory, but facts. Do your own research and you will see. Look at the racial climate here in America when President Obama became the first Black president. And all of the accusations that were railed against him, such as being a Muslim (though he was a Christian) and not being a *true* American.

Look at President Trump's behavior that triggered something in America that was already here.

A man of color becomes president? Some literally lost their minds. Especially, it seemed, that Donald Trump did.

Racism is embedded in a lot of these folks.

Donald is allegedly polarizing and bringing this hidden agenda to the forefront before the others (people of color) totally take over America.

Remember that President Joe Biden selected a woman of color as his running mate (for Vice President) and they won. Now it seemed that made things worse.

Can you imagine what was going through Donald Trump's mind? Did Trump grow up a racist? It was reported that his father had connections to the KKK. There are articles and photographs allegedly showing this connection.

What is the definition of a racist or racism? Do your own research. Remember this slogan: Divide and Conquer!

Judge for yourself!

Who really discovered America, by the way? (Spoiler: it has been reported that it wasn't Christopher Columbus). There are claims from all over the world. If not Columbus, then who?

There are several theories as to who really "discovered" America, some more substantiated than others. According to many articles and information (Wikipedia, Britannica, Library of Congress), Vikings were in America centuries before Columbus got there (before it was ever called America) and there is also evidence (though disputed) that Polynesian explorers visited the continent before the Spaniards did. Technically, Nomadic Asian tribes first discovered America over 15,000 years ago.

But let's take it step by step. The Columbus Expedition

According to the Library of Congress and Britannica, Christopher Columbus departed from the Spanish city of Palos de la Frontera in 1492 with three ships. Ironically, Spanish citizens were forced to contribute to the expedition against their will, although that's the smallest of Columbus' sins.

Fast forward a few weeks, and a lookout sailor on one of the ships saw land. The captain of that ship (not Columbus) confirmed the sighting and alerted Columbus. Seizing the opportunity, Columbus later maintained that he himself had already seen a light hours beforehand -- because the first man to see new land would earn a lifetime pension from the Spanish crown.

As we're already starting to see, Columbus wasn't really the nicest or most honest person. But, apparently the spirit of racism was brought to the establishment of America.

What island they found will remain a question for the ages. What we do know is that Columbus and his crew called it San Salvador; the natives called it Guanahani. It was an island in the Bahamas, but we don't really know which one.

They encountered peaceful natives, who welcomed them peacefully. Columbus noticed the natives were wearing gold bracelets and necklaces, so in true colonial fashion, he took six of them as slaves without hesitation. He wrote in his diary:

"They ought to make good and skilled servants, for they repeat very quickly whatever we say to them. I think they can very easily be made Christians, for they seem to have no religion. If it pleases our Lord, I will take six of them to Your Highnesses when I depart, in order that they may learn our language."

Columbus was also pleased to note that they didn't seem to have any weapons or army. "I could conquer the whole of them with 50 men, and govern them as I pleased." You can see the racist attitude of Christopher Columbus.

What happened later is well-known history. For the locals, it was genocide. For the Europeans of the time, it was a quick way to get incredibly rich and conquer new territories – which they did to the best of their ability.

Judge for yourself.

Some will never admit that many in America still have a racist mentality. Donald Trump allegedly exploited those facts. This is why I gave the history of America earlier.

Yes, it's an ugly history. How people of color were treated, mistreated and looked down upon. Sadly, many still experience this today. As a kid in the South in the late 70s, I was told there were some places of business I shouldn't go in while I was visiting my biological mother in Florida. I was told that they didn't welcome Blacks.

Some towns in America are still like that. Racial profiling and racism still exist. I have experienced it myself many times.

What is the definition of a racist, by the way?

A *racist* is a person who believes in racism: the doctrine that one's own racial group is superior or that a particular racial group is inferior to them.

Again, the key two words are *superior* and *inferior*.

Now I know that's a hard pill to swallow. But it's true.

Some will say, *"Well, how could Donald Trump date women of color?"* Simple. Slave masters were known to have sex with female slaves and father babies.

I went to a non-denominational church where it was forbidden for Blacks to date or marry whites. They believed that interracial marriage was against the Bible. I was young at the time. But when some of the older African American guys displayed an interest in the Caucasian girls, it caused us all to be put out of that Church.

They started an all-Black church for us. And put a Caucasian pastor, who had kids, over it. When the young Black men showed an interest in the white pastor's white girls, they abruptly pulled him and his family out. And put one of the young Blacks who was in his 20s with no pastoral experience over the church.

The church was in disarray and chaotic. I experienced this. I was only 16 or 17 at the time, but I spoke up and said, *this is not right*, during a church meeting.

Prior to the Caucasian overseer leaving with his family, it was very traumatic. Now, I don't have to play the race card. I know the signs and the characteristics of a racist and bigot.

Looking at Donald Trump's past rhetoric and overall attitude, it seems he has a superiority complex. When he was coming down the escalator, talking about Hispanics, etc., and s***hole countries, it's quite clear that he's a person who believes in racism; the doctrine that one's own racial group is superior or that a particular racial group is inferior to the others.

The key words *superior* and *inferior*.

Now I know I gave the definition of a racist twice. But remember the times in which he lived. During the times of segregation and racism. I really can't blame him and others. Because many even in Caucasian-run churches taught racism and were racist. That's what they believed. They believed they were in the dominant race in America. And, therefore, had the God-given authority to enslave the people of color they brought over, fed, and did things for, that they felt was wonderful.

Slavemasters believed in God, but still felt they were superior to people of color. Again I'm not playing the race card. Racism is embedded in those like Donald Trump. He and others can't help themselves because of the way they were raised.

Same with misogyny. Misogyny is the hatred of, contempt for, or prejudice against women or girls. Because there was a time that *women* were viewed as the *lesser being*. It can also refer to social systems or environments where women face hostility and hatred because they're women in a world created by and for men. And these things are historical facts.

The times in which Donald Trump grew up, all these things were acceptable.

Judge for yourself.

SUMMARY

Never underestimate racism nor racist people. Racism is like a cancer that spreads. And, for the most part, has not been diagnosed in people. That is what's needed. Many just don't know they are a racist. Based on what I've read and seen with the Donald, he definitely has racist traits. And I believe it has an underlying spirit behind it. I *do* believe in the spiritual arena. But that's another book.

CHAPTER FIVE

Donald Trump, the Master of Media

Words are powerful and can cause delusion. Donald Trump, is a master of social media, radio and television.

Most don't have a clue how media works nor how to work it. Having done radio for 34 years and television for 24 years, I understand how it's done and I must be honest, Donald is one of the best. Especially when he has an audience. Let me explain.

Whether you're a televangelist, comedian, singer or a motivational speaker, the techniques of public speaking are primarily the same. Especially for those who are effective.

Example: Most Hollywood actors don't just *act* the part. They actually *become* the part in order to connect with their audience. Now, keep in mind, all audience are not the same.

Know your audience and work your role that you're playing.

Again, Donald is a master at that.

He knows triggers and pitch lines to engage and get responses from his supporters. Just look in his crowds and you will see how he uses various words and hand movements. Even on television or radio, if you know what to look for, or listen to, it's an art that can create an illusion.

Example: *They're trying to take over our country. We won't have a country if this continues.*

We won't have a country. Repeat!

What is he really saying? *They*? *They*'re trying to take over our country. Who is *they*? We won't have a country. Who is *we*?

He's not saying, *Make America Great Again*. But make America *what* again? You fill in the blank.

Wow. America has always been a diverse country with certain systems in place to suppress people of color. This is a fact.

There are many hidden agendas at work here and they are not God ordained.

Those who support Donald Trump don't want to lose their supremacy. He is using them so he can have absolute power and authority, in my opinion, by pushing his hidden, divisive agenda. Plain and simple.

Therefore, he uses the media to appeal to those who are his fans, because he is a celebrity to them. He has had an audience for years because of his showmanship tactics. And he seems to have cast a spell over his supporters. It's clear they are overwhelmed with him.

Now, can certain techniques cause hypnotism? Absolutely. Also, temporary insanity and delusions. Watching television, listening to the radio and social media can cause a person to be addicted to certain things and people. And can cause them to become violent based upon what is said.

Yes, I know this may sound crazy. But it's true. Do you not know that manipulation is a form of witchcraft? Even some speakers and preachers use these various techniques. With no sense of compassion or concern for the listener. Only to accomplish their selfish purpose with words and rhetoric that consist of lies that will manipulate those to carry out his diabolical agenda.

Some analysis of Trump's tweets during his presidency found that his most popular and frequent posts largely spread disinformation and distrust (lies). Many of his most-liked tweets contained falsehoods, while the topic he posted about most frequently, "fake news," was a weapon for undermining information. Attack truth by attacking the opposition, as in the news. Especially the networks that fact checked him. In other words, he attacked the messenger.

The system is already in place for mass deception. As I must say, media is a beast, good and bad.

Now calm down for a minute. If there is a man of sin and the antichrist, who in the world has manifested those characteristics, according to the Bible? Truth is hard to accept for some. But not for all of us who know the Bible.

You see, if people would only do their research, regardless of what anyone may be saying, they just might find out they're being lied to or being deceived. When a person operates under the guise of a hidden agenda, watch and listen because they're going to lie and use deception in order to cover it up as an alternative truth.

Many still don’t know how powerful words are. Whether it's a tweet or they are being spoken. It doesn't matter who, or what, it is. Like AI (artificial intelligence) and ChatGPT which are amazing, But I believe is all a part of the antichrist movement or agenda, according to Revelation, chapter 13.

Now I know some don't believe in the Bible or Jesus Christ and definitely not some dictator coming called the antichrist. Well, my advice to you is just to observe what's going on in the world in which we live. Is it possible that the Donald is a part of the fulfillment of Bible prophecy?

Judge for yourself.

SUMMARY

There are all kinds of media sources everywhere. So this is not a hard subject to find data research, etc. Especially when it comes to a celebrity figure like Donald Trump. My main purpose was to show you how powerful all media platforms are. If you don’t know how to work them to your advantage, just look at former President Donald Trump. The media, even social media, is an unbelievable tool, both good and bad. Now we have ChatGPT and AI. Y’all better wake up! Judge for yourself!

CHAPTER SIX

Unmasking / Exposing Deception

Unmasking and exposing deception. How is that really done? What is deception?

There are two words that many are confused by. That is, *deceit* and *deception.* Both nouns, they both loosely describe the act of deceiving (*credit: the dictionary, ELB and other sources*).

The act of deceiving being the act of concealing the truth or otherwise being misleading or false.

In many cases, the words can be used interchangeably. Grammatically speaking, it is rare that you will find a sentence where both words do not fit without the same general meaning. However, the sentences may offer different connotations.

Because, generally speaking, some believe deceit is worse than deception. According to some articles, deceit suggests wickedness, or, more simply, a negative intent.

Deception is more neutral. Though deception, in general, is often connected to negative activities it does not, on its own, suggest wickedness.

Example: a baseball pitcher throws a curve ball instead of a knuckleball. His ability to be deceptive is not wicked. The batter swings, thinking that he's going to get a fastball when it is a curve ball.

Pay close attention to evil and wickedness that's manifested to gain power over people. Apostasy has to do with the church. It is, by definition, the abandonment or renunciation of a religious belief. It's unimaginable how all this is slipping through the cracks.

Here in our country, those who are spiritual men and women should be able to see in the Spirit.

Is this spiritual warfare?

Has Donald Trump released certain spirits over America? And the world?

Now, many really don't want to go there, but evil spirits are real. Could it be that Donald Trump is being influenced by spirits? Or satan himself?

Over the years, many have discounted this phenomenon. I personally believe that demonic spirits are real and can be summoned to act out through people.

That's why some must stand strong and address what's happening. We must not overlook the obvious. The American people aren't ready for what's here and it's not looking good.

Judge for yourself!

SUMMARY

Even though I didn't spend a lot of time on this chapter, I believe you get it. And will do your own research. It's very important that we all judge for ourselves. That's why I refuse to be a Bible thumper. This isn't just based upon those who are claiming to be believers. But anyone can be deceived. The purpose of deceit and deception is for you and me to fulfill someone else's plans. Which can be diabolical or evil. Judge for yourself!

CHAPTER SEVEN

The Spirit of the Antichrist and Donald Trump

In my 40+ years of ministry, I've always been very inquisitive pertaining to the antichrist, end of days, and eschatology. People like Perry Stone, who I had the honor and privilege of meeting and talk to for hours on various subjects as well as listening to his various teaching; Jack Van Impe, another great influence in my life; Irvin Baxter, who I've listened to for hours; as well as Derek Prince, Richard Heard and John Hagee.

These are brilliant minds and I give them credit for challenging my spirit intellectually. Taking notes over the years afforded me the privilege and opportunity to teach on the subject of the antichrist. Why aren't more African-American preachers teaching on this subject? There are some who do, but it takes a lot of time and research.

I shared this with Perry Stone and he said to me that other African-Americans have asked him the same question and he said it would be a blessing. Rabbi Jonathan Cahn, who I also met, was very inspiring to me as I sat and listened to his teaching and took notes. How can you sit in the presence of teachers of this magnitude and not get excited?

Derek Prince, Jack Van Impe, and Irvin Baxter are no longer with us, but their impact is still felt today. Many of us who are students of eschatology may sound like these great men in our writings. What do you expect? It's the same Bible we're using. Revelation 13, by the way, is full of symbolic meaning as well as the books of Ezekiel, Daniel, and Revelation. I often cite those who have influenced me. But the totality will always be what's already written in the Bible. Some of the teachings and writings may not be absolute, but our interpretation of the Scriptures.

Do all of us agree or disagree? No. But many of the symbols have meaning. I've read various articles and I have taken notes. Many things these great men have written about, and lectured on, were already established. Therefore, it's not totally their body of work, but God and those who we believe were inspired by Him.

Teaching on the *spirit* of the antichrist or "the man of sin / the antichrist" is two different subjects. One deals with a broader meaning such as antichrist spirits which are against Jesus Christ. The other is actually a man that embodies not just a spirit, but a demon (or even satan himself).

I believe when reading Revelation 13 again that satan himself takes on the form of a man. There are also several symbolic characters embedded in it which can be compared with references in Daniel 7 (the symbols of the beast, dragon, horns, 10 heads and many animal figures).

Many theologians and scholars have looked deeper into Revelation 13 and Daniel 7. Their findings seem to be an awe moment, or a God moment. Hopefully, my research – as well as the research of others who I have cited in this chapter – will bring a better understanding of the beast, false prophet, symbolic figures and Donald Trump and the role he could play.

The subject of the antichrist could be a book by itself, especially if I included Donald Trump and his ungodly rhetoric and overall behavior. Many accused former Presidents Obama and Reagan, as well as other leaders like Hitler and Popes, as being the antichrist. But now, when looking at Trump, Putin and even the dictators of other countries, it seems the stage is being set for "the Man of Sin" to attempt to rule the world.

As I research other Bible teachers I've seen and heard their unwillingness to even talk about the possibility of former President Trump being a part of this equation. Even though some are dead and gone like Jack Van Impe and Irvin Baxter who would cite President Obama as being a part of the antichrist movement and agenda. Even those like Robert Breaker and John Hagee teaching on the antichrist oftentimes have inserted Obama's name. But I have not once heard them say much about former President Trump and his criminal, totalitarian and ungodly behavior. Remember the Scriptures teaches us that the antichrist is called the "man of sin and the lawless one."

As we look at the Antichrist, or the spirit of the antichrist, we can see all these things coming together especially with the help of Donald Trump, Kim Jong Un, and Putin and a few others. This is unbelievable timing; the way that Donald Trump is acting.

Understanding the biblical imagery of the various symbols in the books of Daniel and Revelation that have been associated with kingdoms, nations and political leaders making a pact, or coalition with major agendas, is helpful. Though it may seem far-fetched, it looks like we are here.

The battle between the kingdom of God and the kingdom of darkness, or satan, is raging in an all-out war. I believe this is because we are nearing the return of Jesus Christ and the ultimate destruction of satan's kingdom.

Looking at the overall operation of this satanic kingdom, the devil, lucifer, satan, or whatever you desire to call him, has always been in opposition to God and those who are a part of the kingdom of God who are fulfilling His purpose in the earth realm. The church of Jesus Christ has always been targeted with various attacks. Let's see how this spirit (antichrist) operates. Looking at the passage in 1 John 2:18–23:

[18] Dear children, this is the last hour; and as you have heard
that the antichrist is coming, even now many antichrists have
come. This is how we know it is the last hour. [19] They went out
from us, but they did not really belong to us. For if they had
belonged to us, they would have remained with us; but their going
showed that none of them belonged to us.

[20] But you have an anointing from the Holy One, and all of
you know the truth. [21] I do not write to you because you do not
know the truth, but because you do know it and because no lie
comes from the truth. [22] Who is the liar? It is whoever denies that
Jesus is the Christ. Such a person is the antichrist – denying the
Father and the Son. [23] No one who denies the Son has the Father;
whoever acknowledges the Son has the Father also.

This text has to do with actions speaking louder than words. The working of the spirit of the antichrist is going to intensify the closer we get to the end of the age.

We must look at the real meaning of the term *antichrist*. The word Christ is from the Greek word, *christos*, which corresponds to the Hebrew word, *Mashiach,* from which we get Messiah. So when we say "antichrist," that means anti-Messiah.

“Anti” has two meanings and both of them apply. First of all, it means “against.” So the first operation is against Messiah. The second meaning is “in place of.” The ultimate purpose is to be a false Messiah in the place of the true Messiah. So the total operation is in two phases.

When talking about the real Jesus Christ, as in separation from the world, some will get upset. That is the spirit of antichrist. But bear in mind that is not the end of satan’s purpose. His purpose is to replace the true Messiah by a false Messiah and false rhetoric.

In 1 John 4:2–3, we read:

“By this you know the Spirit of God: Every spirit that confesses that Jesus [the Messiah] has come in the flesh is of God, and every spirit that does not confess that Jesus [the Messiah] has come in the flesh is not of God. And this is the spirit of the Antichrist, which you have heard was coming, and is now already in the world.”

There are many antichrists who have appeared, and been manifested, in the course of human history.

There is also *the* Antichrist – one specific person – who is the final manifestation of the spirit of antichrist. I believe he’s here, but hasn’t been revealed yet. Time is of the essence. Scripture makes it clear that at the end of this age, there will be one final, evil and powerful ruler, who will dominate the human race for a brief period, who will be *the* Antichrist.

This is very important. Antichrist does not deny the existence of God. In fact, he claims to be God’s representative (as well as claiming to be a god himself). According to 1 John 4, he denies that Messiah has come. He may believe in a Messiah who *will* come, but he denies that Messiah has *already* come. Because he is going to claim to *be* the messiah, though he is an impostor.

[11] Then I saw another beast rising out of the earth. It had two
horns like a lamb and it spoke like a dragon. [12] It exercises all the
authority of the first beast in its presence, and makes the earth and
its inhabitants worship the first beast, whose mortal wound was
healed. [13] It performs great signs, even making fire come down
from heaven to earth in front of people, [14] and by the signs that it
is allowed to work in the presence of the beast it deceives those
who dwell on earth, telling them to make an image for the beast
that was wounded by the sword and yet lived. [15] And it was
allowed to give breath to the image of the beast, so that the image
of the beast might even speak and might cause those who would
not worship the image of the beast to be slain. [16] Also it causes all,
both small and great, both rich and poor, both free and slave, to be
marked on the right hand or the forehead, [17] so that no one can buy
or sell unless he has the mark, that is, the name of the beast or the
number of its name. [18] This calls for wisdom: let the one who has
understanding calculate the number of the beast, for it is the
number of a man, and his number is 666.

—Revelation 13:11–18

John sees a beast rising out of the sea, summoned by the dragon on the seashore (12:17). The vision draws on Daniel 7:3, where Daniel sees "four great beasts . . . out of the sea." The beasts in Daniel are said to represent great empires.

The fourth beast seen by Daniel (Dan. 7:7, 19, 23) is probably the beast in Revelation that has extraordinary power, for it has ten horns, with ten diadems (Rev. 17:12) – symbols of ruling authority – on its horns. It has seven heads, also signifying its authority and power. The dragon had seven heads and ten horns (Rev. 12:3), and he clearly has given his authority to the beast. The beast with its horns and diadems parodies the Christ, just as the dragon does. The seven heads bear blasphemous names, which are perhaps Roman claims to deity, such as "Lord," "son of God," and "Savior," revealing again the divine pretensions of the beast. The beast is not confined to the Roman Empire; it refers to Rome but applies also to every manifestation of evil in all governments throughout history, and also to the final conflict to come at the end.

Take your time to read this (GotQuestions.org). The beast coming out of the sea is like a leopard, with feet like a bear's and a mouth like a lion's. In Daniel's vision of the four beasts, the first (Babylon) was like a lion with eagles' wings (Dan. 7:4), the second (Medio-Persia) was like a bear (Dan. 7:5), and the third (probably Greece) was like a leopard (Dan. 7:6). John sees these beasts consummated in Daniel's fourth beast, which is the beast he describes here (probably Rome). This beast is not autonomous but derives its totalitarian rule from the dragon, and thus its governing authority is demonic.

One of the heads of the beast had a mortal wound, from which it recovered. Many understand this to refer to an individual, which is certainly possible. After Nero's death in AD 68, a tradition arose that he would return (perhaps from Parthia) and rule again, and John might have had that tradition in mind. But if John wrote in the 90s, his most plausible date, it is quite unlikely this tradition would be in mind, since Nero was long gone. It is more probable, then, that the reference is to the empire as a whole. The deadly wound signifies the apparent demise of tyrannical rule. Rome's dominion looks as if it has been dethroned and removed forever. And yet the empire is not destroyed; just when it seems that its tyranny has ended, its power is resumed. The so-called death-blow is ineffective. In response, the world is astonished with the beast and gives its allegiance to him, for the revival of a demonic empire is a kind of resurrection; once again, the beast parodies the Christ.

The staying power of the beast and its empire leads to worship of the dragon and the beast. The dragon is worshiped for giving authority to the beast. The beast is worshiped because of his so-called resurrection. He is considered incomparable and omnipotent, like God. People worship the beast, believing he cannot be resisted or overcome. Is all of this a myth?

You may ask what's the point of referencing the antichrist?

It's the *spirit* of the antichrist that many don't understand. Compare the character of this spirit with the character and Spirit of Jesus Christ. You're not a child of God if you're manifesting the spirit of wickedness and the evil one. Many shall be deceived!

Judge for yourself!

SUMMARY

There's a lot of information out there on the subject of the Antichrist and the spirit of the antichrist. As you can see, many are looking at what's going on in the world today and sounding the alarm. We must not allow ourselves to be blindsided by those who are operating on the behalf of the antichrist, influenced by the *spirit* of this antichrist. Remember, "Anti" means "against" and Christ means *Christo* (Messiah). I believe that from the beginning of time, there have always been intelligent spirits who became evil because of their rebellion against God. These evil spirits will either influence or possess those who are vulnerable and gullible (antichrist). The actual antichrist is noted by some, and the Bible, as being lucifer (morning star) possessing a literal body. It seems like that we will all know sooner than later if the Bible is true. So far, we're seeing Bible prophecy being fulfilled right before our eyes, all around the world. Judge for yourself!

(Limited contributions from these resources: Christianity.com; GotQuestions.org; RonRhodes.org; Smith's Bible Dictionary; and Wikipedia)

CHAPTER EIGHT

God Is In Charge, But He's Given Us Free Will (Control)

What does that mean? I'm glad you asked. That we have the ability to make decisions and are in control of our decisions.

Consider this: God created the whole world from *nothing*. Then he created Adam from the dirt that he created. Think about that: he created Adam from what was *already* created (dirt). But in order for Adam to have life, and become a living soul, God breathed into him the breath of Life.

Now remember Adam and Eve were created in the image and likeness of God (perfect). It's *them* who we're talking about, not us. It takes a man's sperm and a woman's eggs for us to be born into this world. No matter who you are, you were born of a corruptible seed (imperfect), as in egg and sperm, because of the fall (sin, transgression) of Adam and Eve.

Then, after all the animals and other things were created, God saw it wasn't good for man (Adam) to be alone. Especially with all the mating that was probably going on with the animals having other little animals. So God created woman by taking the rib of Adam. Now let me make this plain. God didn't take *your* rib and make a woman. But He took the rib of Adam and made Eve. I believe you got it now. Very simple. Because some have been married two, three, four different times. And if God took a rib every time, you got married again and again and again, you would be in serious trouble.

All of this is written in your Bible. None of us was there, but we choose to believe this documentation by Faith of the Bible.

God gave them both dominion and authority in the Garden of Eden. Keep in mind they had a brain which gave them the ability to name the animals and to do other things. And though God was in charge, He gave them control and management over the garden.

He only gave them one major commandment: *Don't touch nor eat from this one particular tree, or you will die.* (paraphrasing).

You can see how God was in charge, but He gave Adam and Eve control and free will. According to the Scriptures, Adam and Eve violated and disobeyed God's command by listening to the serpent (I believe the serpent was metaphorical). They became the first sinners (transgressors of the Law of God) and were punished for it by being driven out of the garden (Paradise).

There are consequences for those who disobey God. Free will makes everyone individually responsible. When reading Revelation 12 and other Scriptures, you see how lucifer ("morning star," Vulgate) was kicked out of heaven with one third of the angels for attempting to take over the Kingdom of God. He apparently wanted to rule God.

Why was lucifer / satan kicked out of Heaven with a third of the angels who became demons and evil spirits?

Lucifer became so impressed with his own beauty and position that he began to desire the honor that belonged to God. Pride was found in him. And this represents the actual beginning of sin (transgressing the law of God) in the universe – preceding the fall of Adam and Eve.

The serpent was able to influence Adam and Eve to disobey God and obey him (satan). Now keep in mind that they knew no sin; they had never committed sin before. And they were the only ones who were created in God's image and likeness. It's very important you remember that.

You and I were born of a corruptible seed. Therefore we were not created in God's image or His likeness. Because there's no sin in our Creator. Adam and Eve were driven out of the garden because of disobedience. Just like lucifer and the fallen angels were kicked out of Heaven. He was able to deceive and influence God's original creation to disobey their Creator. And that's how sin entered into the world until today.

Now it's up to you and me to be honest with ourselves. Didn't our God give Adam and Eve the right to make *choices* for their lives? You could call it, "the right to *choose*"?

So, why are many playing the role of God, then? If he has given *us* the power of *choice*? God will judge us all based upon our choices.

In the upcoming chapters, you will be able to see how many are influenced by spirits that have caused hypocrisy here in America and in the world. Especially in the Christian community. So, what does it mean when we define America as a Christian country? Now do you see what I'm saying?

When you think about Donald Trump and his Faith, what most people don't understand is, what does he really believe? Does he believe in Faith in Jesus Christ or Faith in Faith?

Consider the teaching of Dr. Norman Vincent Peale who, by the way, was an influencer of the Trump family. One of his main teachings was the power of positive thinking. When I look at his teaching, I see that his premise embodies the theory and concept that Faith in *oneself* is very important (becoming a type of god).

The Greek word for Faith is *pistis*. Which means *trust*. So, what he was allegedly teaching is trust in oneself. Which would be just as powerful as trusting in God. Scripture teaches us in Proverbs 3: 5-6, "Trust in the Lord with all thine heart and lean not unto thine own understanding. In all they ways acknowledge Him, and He shall direct thy paths."

Most people don't understand theology, nor certain erroneous teaching. They claim to be Christians. But don't pursue a better understanding of what it means to be a born-again believer. Trusting Jesus Christ instead of having faith in faith which is not the same as Faith in Jesus Christ. But it is erroneous teaching and heresy.

My endeavor in this chapter is to show you how people use the Bible and words as a tool in order to deceive. Read 2 Corinthians 11:4 where Paul talks about those who will come preaching *another* Jesus, another spirit manifesting itself and another gospel. You can read it for yourself.

As I often say on my various radio talk shows, *Judge for yourself!*

I'm not here to convince you of anything. I'm here to convey information to you. I *do* know some don't have a clue of the spirit world or the spirit I believe is behind Donald Trump. One thing that is obvious is whether he has ever been a humble man like Jesus Christ. But we can see clearly he's lifted up in pride like satan. And that is not an attack. Just listen to the arrogance, lies and vulgarity that comes out of his mouth. That's how you know what's in his heart.

Your Bible teaches that, "out of the abundance of the heart, the mouth speaketh." So, when you hear someone talking consistently about things that are ungodly, it's coming from their heart.

I hope you can see and hear what I'm saying. Now I believe you're getting a better view of what's really in his heart by what he says. Well, does the Donald believe in faith in faith (himself) or Faith in Jesus Christ? Judge for yourself!

SUMMARY

God is still in charge in spite of giving us control. We can see this throughout the Bible, from the beginning of time, regardless of what anyone believes. From lucifer and the fallen angels (who later became satan and demons / evil spirits) according to our Bible that many, including myself, believe in. Even the first man and woman, Adam and Eve, were given the ability, and the opportunity, by their Creator to name the animals and to make their own decisions (control their destiny). But the serpent, who I believe was metaphorical for lucifer / satan / morning star was able to influence them to disobey theirs – and his – Creator. From the beginning of time we can see God didn't create us to be puppets. But there are consequences for our choices. He gave us the ability to choose and be a part of controlling our own destiny. And I honestly believe that. Judge for yourself!

CHAPTER NINE

Lucifer and Mankind; What About Donald Trump?

How do evil spirits operate in the world in which we live?

Is it possible that Donald could be that vehicle and why?

Let's begin by looking at the fall of lucifer (or, morning star) in two Old Testament chapters, Ezekiel 28 and Isaiah 14.

It seems from the context of the first ten verses of Ezekiel 28 that it could be dealing with a human leader. But then, starting in verse 11 and on through verse 19, it seems to be describing lucifer (morning star). Read it for yourself.

The prophet Ezekiel made it clear, the word of the LORD came to me: "Son of man, raise a lamentation over the king of Tyre, and say to him, Thus says the Lord GOD: "You were the signet of perfection, full of wisdom and perfect in beauty. You were in Eden, the garden of God; every precious stone was your covering, sardius, topaz, and diamond, beryl, onyx, and jasper, sapphire, emerald, and carbuncle; and crafted in gold were your settings and your engravings. On the day that you were created they were prepared. You were an anointed guardian cherub. I placed you; you were on the holy mountain of God; in the midst of the stones of fire you walked. You were blameless in your ways from the day you were created, till unrighteousness was found in you. In the abundance of your trade, you were filled with violence in your midst, and you sinned; so I cast you as a profane thing from the mountain of God, and I destroyed you, O guardian cherub, from the midst of the stones of fire.

Your heart was proud because of your beauty; you corrupted your wisdom for the sake of your splendor. I cast you to the ground; I exposed you before kings, to feast their eyes on you. By the multitude of your iniquities, in the unrighteousness of your trade, you profaned your sanctuaries; so I brought fire out from your midst; it consumed you, and I turned you to ashes on the earth in the sight of all who saw you. All who know you among the peoples are appalled at you; you have come to a dreadful end and shall be no more forever." (Ezekiel 28:11-19)

As we move forward in the text, the conclusion from these latter verses seems to refer to the fall of lucifer? Even though the first verses of this chapter speak about the ruler of Tyre (who is rebuked for identifying himself as a god though he was just a man), now it moves to the king of Tyre starting in verse 11. After reading and listening to other scholars who believe that though there was a human "ruler" of Tyre, the real "king" of Tyre was satan, for it was he who was manifesting himself in this ungodly city and it was he who worked through the human ruler of the city.

Some just believe these verses may actually be dealing with a human king of Tyre who was being used by satan. Maybe the king of Tyre was a tool of satan, possibly even being possessed by him.

Whereby there are things that we can see are true of this "king" that cannot be said to be true of human beings. For example, in verse 14, the king seem to have a different nature from man (a cherub); in verse 15, he was blameless and sinless; he was different from an ordinary man (the holy mount of God, verses 13,14); he received a different judgment from man (he was cast out of the mountain of God and thrown to the earth, verse 16). Characteristics describing him don't seem to fit that of a normal human being. It talks about him being "full of wisdom," "perfect in beauty," and having "the seal of perfection" (verse 12 NASB).

When we read the text, it's clear to see that this king was a created being and left the creative hand of God in a perfect state (Ezekiel 28:12-15). And he remained perfect in his ways until iniquity (pride) was found in him (Ezekiel 28:15b). We read in Ezekiel 28:17, "Your heart became proud on account of your beauty, and you corrupted your wisdom because of your splendor." Lucifer apparently became so obsessed with his own beauty and authority he began to desire for himself the position that belonged to God alone. The sin that corrupted lucifer was self-generated pride.

Apparently, this is the beginning of pride. A rebellion that produced sin in the universe before the fall of Adam and Eve. Sin originated in the free will of lucifer apparently.

When we take the time to look at the Scriptures, we see the comparison to many leaders today. It's these *spirits* that are influencing these people. Notice God's response. This mighty angelic being was rightfully judged by God: "I threw you to the earth" (Ezekiel 28:18). This doesn't mean satan had no further access to heaven, for other Scripture verses clearly indicate that satan maintained this access even after his fall (Job 1:6-12; Zechariah 3:1,2). However, Ezekiel 28:18 indicates that satan was absolutely and completely cast out of God's heaven and his place of authority (Luke 10:18).

Isaiah 14, verses 12 through 17, is another Old Testament passage that may also refer to the fall of lucifer. Some argue that the being mentioned in this verse is talking about a man (Isaiah 14:16); who's compared with other kings on the earth (verse 18);

and “How you have fallen from heaven” (verse 12), is alleged to refer to a leader.

"How you are fallen from heaven, O Day Star, son of Dawn! How you are cut down to the ground, you who laid the nations low! You said in your heart, 'I will ascend to heaven; above the stars of God I will set my throne on high; I will sit on the mount of assembly in the far reaches of the north; I will ascend above the heights of the clouds; I will make myself like the Most High.' But you are brought down to Sheol, to the far reaches of the pit. Those who see you will stare at you and ponder over you: 'Is this the man who made the earth tremble, who shook kingdoms, who made the world like a desert and overthrew its cities, who did not let his prisoners go home?' (Isaiah 14:12-17)

There are others who view this passage as referring only to the fall of lucifer.

Now let’s look at another interpretation; that Isaiah 14:12-17 has a *dual* reference. It may be that verses 4 through 11 deal with an actual king of Babylon. Then, in verses 12 through 17, we find a dual reference that includes not just the king of Babylon but a type of depiction of lucifer as well.

Now for those who are born-again believers, you must watch, pray and educate yourselves biblically.

Always remember that satan operates through mankind when it comes to his purpose. Could it be that Donald Trump is a part of that plan? Now this is not an attack on him. But an observation of his behavior and words.

Believing in the coming of the man of sin, or the man of lawlessness (antichrist), according to the Bible, is an interesting subject.

Judge for yourself!

The story of Noah and Sodom and Gomorrah are very interesting stories. Because they both deal with God's judgment. Now some who don't believe in the Bible, this is not for you. This is for Donald Trump and his Christian followers Regardless of God's love for mankind, he never tried to make anyone serve or obey him. He gave Adam and Eve his commandment in the Garden, but he didn't force them to keep it. He told them about the consequences.

As in the Days of Noah

120 years of preaching the Judgment of God it was going to rain 40 days and nights when it had never rained before (consequences), but never forcing anyone to enter the Ark. By the way, only eight entered. And those were Noah's family.

Sodom and Gomorrah

Abraham stood as an intercessor (a person who intervenes on behalf of another or others, especially by prayer). But the people rejected the notion that an intercessor was needed to appeal to God to not destroy their region. And God went from, "If I can find 50 to how many righteous people?" Five. But He found none.

And then He walked away. He never forced anyone to serve Him. Nor did He give anyone the authority to execute judgment on anyone who didn't believe in Him or His judgment. Only four left the cities of Sodom. God honored Abraham and allowed his nephew Lot and family to be escorted out of the city by angels before the fire and brimstone started falling. They were all told not to look back. But Lot's wife did and she was turned into a pillar of salt. Did God force them – or her – to do anything? No.

Did God give Adam and Eve free will? Didn't God give those in the days of Noah and Sodom free will? Well, didn't Jesus Christ give all free will when He said, "Whosoever will, let him come?"

What about, "For God so loved the world, that He gave his only begotten Son that whosoever believeth in Him should not perish, but have everlasting life?"

What about, "Choose ye this day whom you will serve?"

Judge for yourself!

SUMMARY

Ask yourself, who is lucifer (morning star) and what is his agenda if he does exist? What about mankind, Adam and Eve, who are mentioned in Genesis? Is this a true story or made up by men? Some believe it is true. We do know Donald Trump is real and we can all see his behavior whether some are willing to acknowledge that or not. The existence of lucifer doesn't exist in the minds of many. But that doesn't mean he doesn't exist. There is a spiritual world out there that I believe really exists. My writing on this subject is to convey and not to convince. Judge for yourself!

(Limited contributions from these resources: BibleGateway.com; BibleHub.com; GotQuestions.org; and Wikipedia)

CHAPTER TEN

Abortion and Same Sex Relationships

According to the Bible, these things go against God's order of creation and our Christian Faith. But do we have the right to dictate and control people's choices? God didn't even do that. He gave people the right to choose.

What about Jesus Christ? Did He force people to serve or live for Him?

It's amazing how Christians ignore this main factor about God. Do they even know God? Have they even read the Scriptures where all humanity is given the ability to make their own choices?

Adam and Eve made their own choices. Lucifer (morning star) and one-third of the angels made their choice. All mankind has the same options. But there are consequences to their choices.

Because of the fall of Adam and Eve, in the beginning, we were all born into sin and shaped into iniquity. We live in a fallen world. In other words, we came out of the womb as sinners. This is why we all need to be born again.

Abortion is a choice. Same-sex marriage is a choice. Just like I choose to surrender to Jesus Christ. There are laws of the land that we must abide by or suffer the consequences. Just like the law of God. If we don't abide by them, there are consequences.

But you and I have no right to control anyone's choices. God gave them the right to choose. All mankind has the right to choose whether to serve Jesus Christ or not. We must continue to teach and preach the gospel of Jesus Christ and the consequences of violating the commandments of God.

What is an Evangelical? What is the difference between Evangelicals and Protestants? All are under the umbrella of Christianity.

Evangelicals are a subgroup of Protestants who emphasize the authority of the Bible and the importance of personal conversion. They tend to be more conservative in their theology and social beliefs than other branches of Christianity.

Protestant churches predominantly have a liberal theology while evangelical churches tend to have a more fundamentalist or moderate conservative theology. Some commentators have complained that Evangelicalism, as a movement, is too broad and its definition too vague to be of any practical value. (let me be fair: not *all* evangelicals support Donald Trump; and there are some more liberal Protestants who *do* support him.)

So is Donald Trump really an evangelical? Read below what evangelicals are supposed to believe and teach.

According to their Statement of Faith (as adopted by the National Association of Evangelicals, on their website), evangelicals believe:

1. The Bible is the inspired, infallible, and authoritative Word of God. This underscores the high regard evangelicals hold for Scriptures, although individual churches and denominations may differ in the interpretation of specific passages.

2. There is one God, eternally existent in three persons: Father, Son, and Holy Spirit. Evangelicals tend to interpret the doctrine of the Trinity literally and ascribe utmost importance to this belief.

3. Jesus Christ is the divine Son of God, born of a virgin, leading a sinless life, performing miracles, dying vicariously and atoning for sins through His shed blood, rising bodily from the dead, ascending to the right hand of the Father, and promising His return in power and glory. These events are considered essential, historical, and literal by evangelicals.

4. Regeneration by the Holy Spirit is crucial for the salvation of lost and sinful individuals. This belief emphasizes the role of the Holy Spirit indwelling believers upon their faith in Christ. It does not align explicitly with the Calvinist-Arminian debates but embraces a broad understanding.

5. The present ministry of the Holy Spirit enables Christians, through His indwelling, to live a godly life. While acknowledging that Christians may still sin, evangelicals believe that the Holy Spirit empowers believers to live in accordance with godly principles.

6. Both the saved and the lost will experience resurrection—those saved will rise to eternal life, while those lost will rise to eternal damnation. This reflects the belief in an afterlife with eternal consequences.

7. Believers in Jesus Christ, regardless of denominational affiliation, are spiritually united. Despite theological differences, evangelicals believe that true faith in Christ unites all believers.

This unity extends beyond the confines of evangelicalism, encompassing all those who genuinely place their faith in Christ, forming a universal church.

Now you know. So, concerning some of the followers of Donald Trump, are they *really* Evangelicals?

America, the Christian country, and Donald Trump, the 21st century savior of the world?

Everything that is written, or will be written, you must judge for yourself and do your own research.

What is America? Very simple answer. It's a capitalistic country made up of all types of people and religions. Have you ever researched the history of America? Was it discovered by Christopher Columbus? Were there people here before?

Before you accuse me of hating America and Donald Trump and tell me to go back to Africa where I came from, use your brain. First of all, I never came from Africa. Just like you never came from where your ancestors come from. Now, who was here before our ancestors?

After reading information about the origins of America, when I hear the expression, "America is a Christian country," I have to ask, "Is America a *godly* Country?"

Now when we say, "country," shouldn't we be focusing on the people? Fifty years ago, 90% of Americans identified as being Christians. By 2021, only 63% make the same claim.

Many non-Christians have studied the Bible in order to prove that those who claim to be of the Christian faith don't practice what they preach. Apparently, Donald Trump is taking advantage of this hypocrisy.

Why don't people and the Evangelicals see what's really going on in the spiritual realm? Donald Trump allegedly desires to rule the world. I have heard him speak on several occasions concerning himself being the answer for all the problems in the world.

Don't you see the sovereignty of God throughout the Bible? Are Evangelicals and many Christians trying to play God? Or, at least trying to fill the role?

By the way, I'm a preacher of righteousness. But if a man or woman decides they are gay or want to live a gay lifestyle, that's their choice. Same for abortions. Our Creator has given us the choice to choose, according to what I read in my Bible. Yes, there are consequences to your choices. Good or bad. Heaven or hell. And it's not just same-sex relationships and abortions that will bring about judgment or damnation.

Who is the father of lies? Who have we seen on television, heard on radio, and read tweets for the past several years, who has lied more openly than anyone I have ever known? And who is a champion for the Evangelicals and Christians? Now I’m not saying that other politicians, and other people, don’t lie. But, as the President of the United States of America, life is not a joke.

I believe America is a Christian country, but is it a godly Country?

As God gave Jezebel a space for repentance, I believe that Donald Trump and many others need to manifest repentance toward God.

No, I don't believe the Bible is for same-sex marriages or abortions. The Bible doesn't condone sin in general. We live in a fallen world. Thank God for the blood and the sacrifice of Jesus Christ for our redemption and salvation. But in spite of all that Jesus Christ did, it is our choice to serve him or not. We must stop and not be hypocrites when it comes to other people.

SUMMARY

Now I personally am not for abortion or same-sex unions. But I am also not for controlling anyone's choices and decisions. I understand clearly that Jesus Christ did not give anyone the authority to dictate, control, or punish anyone for their decisions in this life. As it was in the days of Noah, and Sodom and Gomorrah, so shall it be in the last days. So my mindset is to just allow things to take their course. Same-sex relationships, according to the Bible, had a lot to do with what took place in Sodom and Gomorrah. It seems that Bible prophecy, as I said before, is being fulfilled. Do your own research and judge for yourself!

CHAPTER ELEVEN

The Human Character of Jesus Christ Compared to the Character of Donald Trump

Let us look at the character of Jesus Christ, who became our example as a human being, knowing we lived in a fallen world.

Jesus, as a human, was very compassionate. He manifested compassion consistently by feeding the homeless, healing those who were sick and teaching us how we should treat one another. Whenever people were around him, Jesus discerned their needs and sought to address them. For some, physical healing was necessary. For others, their need was spiritual. In all cases, Jesus took the time to help hurting people.

It's quite clear that Jesus had a love for others. He couldn't be compassionate or a servant without loving people. Jesus said that there is no greater love than for a man to lay down his life for a friend, and we should lay down our life for one another. He did just that for us. If anyone doubts His love, all they have to do is look upon the cross and see the agony that He bore for their sins. He experienced that horrible death so that *all* could be saved.

Jesus was forgiving. One of the most powerful manifestations of this is found in Luke 23:34, when Jesus is on the cross and He proclaims: "Father, forgive them, for they know not what they are doing." Even bleeding and experiencing excruciating pain, Jesus had His heart set on forgiving those who wanted Him to die. This is contrary to today's attitude of looking out for *self*. Jesus was by no means concerned for His own life; all He wanted was to provide a way for forgiveness. That's why He laid down His life.

Jesus was fully committed to the purpose of the Father. Despite praying fervently in the garden of Gethsemane to avoid having to bear the cross and all that physical torture, He knew it was the only way to pay for everyone's sins. He knew He had to be crucified for the sins of the world.

Jesus prayed constantly. He always found time to be alone with God to communicate with Him. Whether in the garden of Gethsemane, across a river, or on a mountaintop, Jesus would disappear for a while to pray. He made sure to make time with His heavenly Father a priority, in spite of being God manifested in the flesh.

Jesus was gentle. Although there were certain times when Jesus became upset, He knew when gentleness was needed. Children seemed to love coming to Him, and He made sure the disciples knew that. When speaking with His disciples, His mother, or others, He was very kindhearted and gentle. But, when rebuking those who opposed truth, or when making a point in an argument, He was very stern with no apology.

Jesus was patient. He knew that He had to be to fulfill the purpose of God. He was surrounded by disciples who doubted Him, Pharisees and Sadducees who attacked Him, and large crowds of people who were broken, hungry and needed healing. Despite all of that, He stayed focused and helped them.

Jesus exercised self-control. He was even tempted of the devil, without sin. He was offered many things in the world as a man. But the purpose of God was greater than having this world's possessions. And He submitted His total life as a man to the will of the Father. I'm quite sure He had desires for food when He fasted 40 days and nights, but He was on a mission for the Lord to accomplish what He set out to do.

Jesus was humble. In whatever He was doing – His teachings and all His miracles – He never made it about Himself. It was always for others and to the glory of God. Even when the crowds sought to make Him their king – in other words, their physical king – He didn't entertain any of that. He refused to be a dictator. He understood the purpose, the mission, and the assignment. And that was to be an example to mankind. His main objective was to destroy the works of the devil so that men, women, boys and girls could be saved and not lost. He was about the purpose of God and the saving of those who were lost.

In spite of Jesus being God manifested in the flesh on Earth, He became our example, manifesting characteristics such as humility, self-control, patience, gentleness, prayerfulness, forgiveness, and commitment. And we should all follow His lead. But you can't do that unless you deny yourself.

You see, the world doesn't need more celebrities. It needs more of us to manifest the character of Jesus Christ. We won't find a better person than Jesus Christ as an example. He showed us what it meant to be compassionate, considerate, kind and loving. He was willing to deny Himself. And that is what we all should be willing to do. For the Bible says, Jesus said unto His disciples, if any man will come after me, let him deny himself, and take up his cross, and follow me.

Now when we look at the character of Donald Trump, we must not look at how he was born in wealth, privileged, but how he has handled people over the years.

Look how he was sued by the federal government for housing discrimination, with his father; how he allegedly mistreated the women he married; how he allegedly didn't pay many of his workers while making money for himself; how his investments caused other people to invest, but when they lost their money, he made no restitution for them. Many of his businesses failed due to lack of honesty and transparency and shady dealings. Later on, prior to becoming the president of the United States of America, he had other suspicious business deals going on at the time.

After running for president of the United States, he openly made fun of a handicapped individual; incited violence from his followers at some of his rallies; and made fun of women, talking about their weight and their looks. We have seen the former president become angry, hateful and ungodly when things don't go his way (retaliation). He has also allegedly told countless lies.

Who is the father of lies? I'm glad you asked. satan. And who has demonstrated the mindset of a child, in public? The Bible tells us, Paul said, "when I was a child, I behaved like a child, but when I became a man, I put away childish things."

Trump blamed the general decline of Atlantic City for his company's failures, although critics pointed out that his casinos had never done well, even when Atlantic City's gambling economy had been strong. Allegedly, he lied about that. Efforts to revive the company failed, and it seemed it caused him to enter into bankruptcy again in 2009 and 2014, a few years before he ran for the highest office in the land. By the time Trump announced his campaign for president in 2015, his gambling businesses had ceased operation entirely. Shareholders in the company lost their investments, and many vendors and creditors suffered losses, but Trump's personal financial losses were mitigated by his financial and legal actions. What would Jesus do?

During his business career, Donald Trump retained the public appearance of success. As his real estate and gambling businesses failed, he succeeded in protecting his brand and shifted into licensing businesses in the United States and abroad. In 2004, the New York Times noted: "His name has become such a byword for success that even the most humiliating reverses barely dent his reputation. Apparently, the rules that govern others just don't apply to Donald Trump." A good name is better than rubies.

Therefore, that tells us, not just about him, but about his followers. And those who ignore his behavior. And will vote him back into the presidency again, if possible. In spite of the Capitol, the insurrection; in spite of his rhetoric, praising Putin, and the dictator of North Korea. Judge for yourself. Look at yourself in the mirror. Do you teach your kids to be like this?

This is not a bashing of Donald Trump. It's just looking at what he lacks; the character of Jesus Christ. The same could be said for some of the people who follow him. What kind of example has "the Donald" portrayed over his 70 years of life, and being a president or former president?

According to my research and observation of "the Donald," I see a man full of hatred and greed, full of himself; a wannabe dictator who loves money and power. And just think about it: America's electoral college voted him president of the United States not long ago. But America is a Christian country?

Now, with all that's been said – time will not allow me to go over all the articles out there, from the Washington Post, The New York Times, USA Today, and all other media outlets – about all the combativeness, all the name calling, all the lies that have been told; all the corruption that we see; deceit, deception, insulting women, by one man. You may say, *don't all politicians lie?* We have never had a politician like Donald Trump. You can judge it for yourself.

SUMMARY

Many who claim to be of the Christian faith seem to ignore the character of Jesus Christ. In our comparison of Donald Trump and the life of Jesus Christ, you see we must be honest with ourselves. Look up the definition of character. If you, me, or Donald Trump are servants of Jesus Christ, don't you think we should be concerned about reflecting His character (Jesus Christ) and not something else? Yes, baby saints do need to be nurtured and discipled. But we must stop making excuses for ourselves and "the Donald." Keep in mind that we all should become more like Jesus Christ. Anything less than that is a clear sign of a lack of surrender to Jesus Christ. And, of course, no Servants of Jesus Christ should be retaliating against others, or holding grudges. Neither are they crooked and carnal, but loving, considerate of everyone which is very important. We all should become more like Jesus Christ in all that we do. Teaching is very important, especially to those who identify as being Christians. Judge for yourself!

CHAPTER TWELVE

Donald Trump, from Businessman to the 45th President

How did he do it?

As we look at his life history, since 1968, which is an amazing story, we can see that he was apparently raised in a very ambitious family. It's quite clear to see the lifelong patterns he lived by, and operated by, as a businessman.

Not only that, but having the ability to establish various companies and wealth is remarkable in itself. He also built over the years a celebrity name brand (Trump) and he licensed the name.

Most Americans were so impressed with him, that literally millions voted for him to become the president. The conditions of the world and America at the time were ripe for a man like "the Donald" who is more of a celebrity and entertainment-driven person than a politician who understands policies and politics.

I am convinced that being a television / radio personality, having money, and being a global iconic figure, opened the door of opportunity for him to become the 45th president of the United States of America, whether qualified or not. We see how Donald, as president of the United States of America, has been seen and heard by billions, holding the highest office in the most powerful country in the world. And now he's trying to obtain it again.

"The Donald" has never worked for anyone but his father and himself. With that being said, we read and see all the corruption that many thought were legitimate businesses prior, also articles about his family, racism, his attitude toward people of color, and how he allegedly wanted the Central Park Five, young African-

American boys, to be executed for a crime they were found innocent of.

Also his many lies that he has allegedly told over the years. All this you can find if you only do your own research. I give credit to all who have written books, articles and lectures about the former president.

I believe there's a spirit (antichrist) behind him that has influenced him and others. It seems as if the end is near, according to Bible prophecy, that many just don't believe in. The world seems to be headed towards self-implosion, which will set the stage for a one-world government and a one-world belief system (religion).

And the Antichrist, a one-world ruler, who will come on the scene and promise that he can solve all the problems in the world.

Now this is not bashing Donald Trump, but it's quite interesting to have heard what has come out of his mouth at many of his rallies.

Revelation 13 is a good read if you will use certain commentaries and listen to certain men and women on the subject of the antichrist.

Educate yourself on Donald's life history of faith, business dealings and branding. His ability to market his name. Which was more important than all of his businesses. I believe this is how he became the 45th President in spite of failed businesses, marriages and what we call negative publicity. It's how he has used his fame, to become a household name.

There will always be people out there who will support him and even die for him. I believe now you see Donald Trump's path to POTUS thanks to his Dad, Fred, and Dr. Norman Vincent Peale, who gave him the tools as a kid to become the most powerful man in the world. It will be very interesting how all of this we see will end. With all of the indictments, with all the corruption and bad behavior, with all the attacks, the insults, and just straight-up nonsense that this man has displayed for the whole world to see. Judge for yourself!

SUMMARY

As we move into this uncertain season in the world in which we live, Bible prophecy is being fulfilled. I personally feel the stage has been set for "the Man of Sin" (the antichrist). Am I saying that Donald Trump is that man? No, but with everything that has happened, and that is happening, he could be a forerunner who has prepared the way for that diabolical figure. We must watch, pray and prepare. As well as speak what the Bible says will take place in the last days. Are we here? Judge for yourself!

CHAPTER THIRTEEN

The Danger That Comes with The Power of Positive Thinking When It Excludes Jesus Christ

Now, how is it possible to play on people's emotions? And to get them to do and believe whatever you say?

After years of studying human behavior and triggers that cause certain emotional responses, let me expose the art of how Donald allegedly operates as a victim to most Evangelicals; as well as those who say they believe in Christianity, but don't practice it; and those who don't even believe in Jesus Christ. It all has to do with a person being able to connect with individuals and persuade them to embrace their rhetoric or their agenda.

Claiming to be a Christian is not the same as the practice of applying Christian values to one's life. I hear these words thrown around constantly, *I'm a Christian*.

But, what does that *mean*? What *are* Christian values that people are talking about? What are *your* Christian values? Can you define them? Can you name them? Can Donald Trump tell you what they are?

When Donald says, I'm fighting for your Christian values; I'm your leader; I'm the one that's going to protect you; I can fix it; I can stop wars, poverty and bring back financial security, but the far left and the liberals want to demonize me and all I'm trying to do is help you. What is he saying? Is he saying, I'm your messiah, or savior? The word messiah means savior. One who is able to deliver you and save you from your enemies. He says, look at what I'm going through for you. Just like Jesus. And he has implied that.

Look at the big picture.

Donald is a professional actor / performer, when it comes to playing the victim. That's a maneuver technique that he and others use to get sympathy and support. Even though they may bring things on themselves. They've learned how to tap into the emotions of people. His teaching molded his thoughts to believe you have the ability to create whatever you desire. Just like lucifer (morning star) thought. And he was able to influence one-third of the angels who were with God in Heaven in the Beginning.

Words are powerful and have the power to hypnotize the masses. That's right. Do you not know that some practice hypnosis by using words? Do your own research and you will see what I'm saying.

Listen closely to what Trump says to his millions of followers. He is a prolific showman and communicator.

There's a connection between Noah, Lot, Donald Trump and all that's going on in our world today. And it's called *The Last Days*. As it was in the days of Noah, as it was in the days of Lot, so shall it be when the Son of Man returns. As we pray and intercede for our world, read Genesis 18:16-33, where Abraham pleads with God for the city of Sodom and Gomorrah.

As we can clearly see in Genesis 18:17, the honor and the respect that God shows Abraham, who is known as a friend of God. When Abraham not only prays to Him, but pleads with God to have mercy on Sodom and Gomorrah as well as the other cities around, because of their defiance and outright rebellion toward God. When God saw all of this Himself, Abraham knew the cities where doomed. But because of his relationship with Him, he pleaded for mercy for this ungodly region.

God and him agreed on, if he could find 50 righteous people, He wouldn't destroy the cities, but He couldn't find them in the whole region. Okay, what about 45... 40... 30... the number went all the way down to five righteous people in order to spare the region. Then, as we can see, He just walked away after none could be found.

We see how kind and merciful God is. Knowing that the people refused to put forth any effort of repentance and the acknowledgement of His mercy and grace. Only Lot, his wife and two daughters were blessed to leave because of Abraham.

The only thing left for us to do today is for everyone to manifest repentance in this hour in which we live. As we see the mercy and the grace of God when it came to Abraham interceding for the cities of Sodom and Gomorrah, we should have a change of heart and direction. And that is what repentance is all about: a change of heart and change of direction. God is full of love, grace and mercy. But there are consequences for our choices, both good and bad.

Eternity is forever. The stage and climate is set for what's next. Who knows? It seems that the Judgment of God has been unleashed already: the weather, wars and rumors of wars, civil unrest, the falling away in the Church (faith in Jesus Christ is less than it has ever been), false teachers, false prophets everywhere. The Bible is being fulfilled right in front of us. Think about it.

And now we have a former president who's been indicted four times. And he and his followers have caused an uproar and chaos (they stormed the Capitol).

Things are going to get worse. Like the Bible tells us. All these things must come to pass. Stay alert. Don't lose faith in Jesus Christ. Because He has the last say.

And pray for Donald Trump, and the world, that they would all find Jesus if they don't know Him.

As you glean over Donald Trump's teaching, and what he has been taught, I'm quite sure now you can see the danger of the teaching that he was exposed to. Even as a child. He was so overwhelmed at six years old, articles stated, with the teachings of Dr. Norman Vincent Peale that he would make comments to his family concerning that teaching. You can be whatever you want to be. You can do whatever. It's all based upon your thought process. And it will happen. Absolutely.

This is why in many of the chapters it might seem that I was repeating myself. I am. It's intentional.

I challenge you to read 2 Corinthians, chapter 11. Read the whole chapter. Especially verses 2 through 4.

And pray for Donald Trump, and the world, that they will find Jesus Christ before it's too late.

May God Bless You!

SUMMARY

The teaching on The Power of Positive Thinking by Dr. Norman Vincent Peale, as well as his books and lectures, I believe molded “the Donald's” life. When a teaching is more about one’s self instead of Jesus Christ, that's a cause for concern. After reading the various chapters of this book, I hope and pray that you see the need for Donald Trump to have a real relationship with Jesus Christ. And not only the former president, but the entire country needs to turn to Jesus Christ. With all the various teaching and religious theories and concepts, we must make sure that we're not being deceived. Judge for yourself!

The Conclusion

As I look around at all that's happening in the world, I can't help but believe there's something in the air.

The worst pandemic in our lifetime. God is the one who sends plagues as a type of judgment.

The Bible speaks about climate change, wars, people turning against each other, alternative lifestyles, love growing cold, lawlessness, perilous times.

The Bible says, as it was in the days of Noah and Lot, these things that we are seeing, must come to pass.

All of these things are ripe for a man like Donald Trump (chaos) – even though he's no longer the president – and his administration, especially if he's re-elected. Regardless of how people may feel, he could win the presidency again. I believe he has a very strong spirit behind him (satan) that many are not ready for.

He has displayed ungodly behavior and an ungodly attitude; showed disrespect towards women and other people, and yet some people are still willing to support him. Who would vote for a man like that? Only God knows.

But God said, there will come a time that the man of sin, the lawless one, the antichrist, would come on the scene and deceive the whole world.

I'm not saying that Donald Trump is the antichrist. But I am saying, looking at the characteristics of the antichrist (who will be a dictator) and listening to what comes out of Donald Trump's mouth, on a consistent basis, it should cause all of us to be concerned.

Lord have mercy as I prepare for the Will of God. And what's here.

SUMMARY

Many don't have a clue of what's going on in the world. Bible prophecy is being fulfilled right before our eyes. The war in Israel; the conflict in Ukraine with Russia; China, North Korea and those countries that hate Israel; are all signs of what the Bible calls the "last days" or "end times." If you have never read Matthew 24, Revelation 12 and 13, or Daniel 7 and Ezekiel 36-38, I encourage you to do so. We must get the biblical information out there. I have done years of research, reading books, listening to lectures from great teachers. Many contributors and mentors have passed away. But I am thankful for their influence on my life that challenged me and my willingness to research and write about such a must-needed book: Donald Trump: Servant of Jesus Christ, or of satan? Judge for yourself!